GRIZZLY CUB

GRIZZLY CUB

Five Years in the Life of a Bear

∎

RICK MCINTYRE

ALASKA NORTHWEST BOOKS™

ANCHORAGE ▪ SEATTLE

*For bears everywhere, and for those
humans who are on their side.*

Library of Congress Cataloging-in-Publication Data
McIntyre, Rick.
Grizzly cub: five years in the life of a bear/by Rick McIntyre
p.   cm.
ISBN 0-88240-373-7
1. Grizzly bear — Alaska — Denali National Park and Preserve.
2. Grizzly bear — Alaska — Denali National Park and Preserve — Infancy.
I. Title.
QL737.C27M359   1990   90-35587
599.74'446—dc20
CIP

Edited by Randy Michael Signor and Marlene Blessing
Design by Elizabeth Watson
Photos by Rick McIntyre

Alaska Northwest Books™
A division of GTE Discovery Publications, Inc.
22026 20th Avenue S.E.
Bothell, Washington 98021

PREFACE

There is something about a grizzly bear, something that sets it apart from all other animals.

That was how I felt when I was a kid, growing up in Massachusetts. Every time a grizzly appeared on TV or in a movie, I stared at it and wondered about being close to a real one. I never expected to be near one, but it was fun to think about.

Ten years later, I enrolled at the University of Massachusetts and chose forestry as my major. During the next three summers, I worked in the White Mountain National Forest in New Hampshire. After college, I worked in California as a fire fighter for the National Park Service at Kings Canyon National Park.

That was where I first saw black bears. I was excited to finally see a live, wild bear, but a part of me believed that it still wasn't the same as seeing a grizzly. I wanted to go to Alaska, in particular, to Denali National Park. I heard you could see grizzlies there every day.

I kept my eyes open, and in the spring of 1976, I was offered a summer job in Denali as a seasonal naturalist. Immediately after arriving in Denali, I joined the rest of the new employees on an orientation tour into the park. About an hour into the trip, the ranger conducting the tour stopped the bus and told us to look to our right. And up on a hillside, about a half mile from the bus, I saw a mother grizzly and two cubs digging peacefully for roots; after a minute, they wandered over the hill and disappeared from view.

They were my first grizzlies. Although the bears looked big and powerful, I was more impressed that day with how gentle they seemed. The bears I saw were nothing like the rampaging grizzlies portrayed in movies.

I was assigned to live at Eielson Visitor Center, sixty-five miles out in the park. My duties involved staffing the center and leading nature walks, campfire talks, and conducting other naturalist programs. Eielson was located in one of the best areas in the park to see grizzlies. Often, we spotted grizzlies from the visitor-center windows. Sometimes bears walked across the clearing and passed near the building. Once, one looked in my bedroom window, left a big nose print on the glass, and sauntered away. I saw grizzlies even more frequently when I was off duty, out looking for wildlife.

The stories were true: you could see grizzlies every day in Denali.

The open expanse of the tundra enabled me to watch bears go about their business even if they were miles away. I found the frequency of sightings never lessened my interest in them.

The summer ended and with it the job. I hadn't yet seen enough grizzlies, so I decided to return for another season next year.

Many more summers came and went, and each new season I learned a little more about grizzlies. My only regret was that I hadn't seen many cubs close enough to study grizzly family relationships.

That all changed in 1984, my ninth summer at Denali. I encountered a tiny cub that year who was to become a familiar sight for several years to come. The cub, whom I called Little Stony, made a permanent impression on me, and eventually broadened my knowledge of the nature of grizzlies.

I decided to write a biography of Little Stony so I could share his unique life with others. Although the story takes place in Denali National Park, the central elements of this cub's life relate to all national parks, because the events of Little Stony's life illustrate how difficult it is to strike the proper balance between preservation of a natural area and use of the same area by humans.

CONTENTS

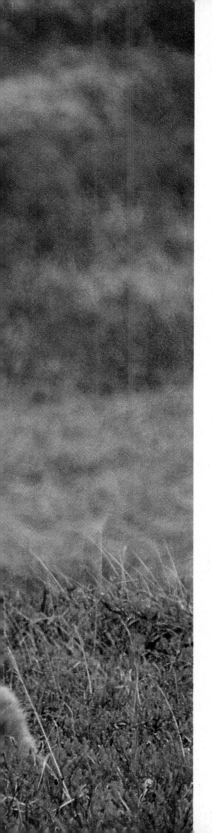

YEAR 1 ONE

. . . .

When I first saw him, he was the size of a teddy bear. The tiny grizzly cub stood beside the road and stared at me as I coasted the truck to a stop. He continued to look at me for a few more moments before dashing off to catch up with his mother. The two grizzlies crossed the road, passing within yards of my truck.

I had never been so close to

Mother and cub in a rare play session.

11

such a young cub. The two bears stayed near the road for the rest of the day, and I spent ten hours watching them.

The cub was only five months old, but already he had a well-developed personality. He played continuously, his play fueled by tireless curiosity about his world.

Everything on the tundra was a potential toy. He picked up a rock that interested him and carried it around in his jaws. Then he attacked a willow bush he came upon, and climbed it until it dumped him on the ground. A second assault got him a little higher, but he soon lost his balance and started to slip. As he fell, he grabbed a branch with his teeth. For several moments he dangled by his jaws from the branch while he struggled furiously to swing himself back up. The branch broke and he tumbled to the ground. Sprawled on his back, he suddenly realized he could turn the broken branch into a toy. The cub juggled the branch, first with his front paws and then with his back feet. When this no longer held his interest, he stood on his hind legs and carried the branch around in his jaws.

But the plaything that best showcased his exuberant curiosity was a snowbank. It took the cub a few tries, but he finally figured out that by sitting down he could slide down the bank — which he did, repeatedly, racing back to the top of the snowbank, sitting on his haunches, and spinning down the snowy slope.

Little Stony's distinctive white fur necklace makes him easy to identify.

. . . .

Though the cub's inventiveness enabled him to play for hours with things he found on the tundra, eventually he grew bored and looked for a playmate. Since he had no siblings, his choice was limited to one: his mother. His next problem was how to interest her.

He ran up to her and bit her on the cheek. She ignored the cub

The cub tries to get his mother to play, but she merely steps over him and walks away.

The sow brings
Little Stony to his first
bear flower patch, a
delicacy that quickly
becomes one of his
favorite foods.

. . . .

and continued to feed. The cub then stood directly in front of her, blocking her path. Without taking any apparent notice, she bowled him over and resumed grazing. She had sent him tumbling down a hillside, but he jumped up and ran back for a second try. This time he slipped beneath her hind legs, walked under her belly, and then pushed his way between his mother's jaws and the food she sought. He rolled on his back, wiggled his four paws in the air, and tried to bite her chin. This also failed to elicit any response. When the sow walked off, he ran after her and fiercely attacked her hind legs. She was oblivious to this assault as well and continued feeding.

Next the cub ran up to her, swatted her in the face, and immediately dashed off. Stopping forty feet away, he looked back to see if his blow had provoked a reaction. If he had done that to another bear cub, it would have sparked a furious game of run-and-chase across the tundra. She was still peacefully feeding, however, paying no attention to him.

The mother bear was determined to eat, while the cub was equally determined to play. All of his schemes and tricks were ignored. The mother seemed too dignified to get involved with something as frivolous as play.

After several hours of this, the sow stopped her feeding and yielded to the cub's incessant demands. She sat down and lowered her

How can any mother ignore such a cute cub?

When the cub finishes this nursing session, he discovers that his mother has fallen asleep. Taking advantage of her warm, soft stomach, he curls up on top of her and dozes off.

head to his level. He bit and bashed her face, ears, and neck. She nipped back gently. The cub stood and attacked the fur on her cheeks. He then rolled onto his back and the sow pretended to attack him, which then enabled him to counterattack her face and chest. Sometimes their bites looked fierce: but much the way the family dog romps and mock-bites when playing with children, the two bears seemed to know just how much force to use with each other.

After five minutes of play, the mother rolled onto her back and

18

nursed the cub. A few minutes later, the tired but satisfied cub began a well-deserved nap.

It was not destined to be a restful sleep. A few minutes after dozing off, the cub opened an eye and looked for his mother. She was forty-five feet away, chewing on a fresh patch of grass. Afraid of being left behind, he jumped up and ran toward her. Once he was next to her, he lay down again and resumed his nap. Not much later he looked up and found that he had been abandoned again. He rushed to catch up. This time he bedded down right under her stomach. When the sow moved on, she had to lift a hind leg over the cub to avoid stepping on him. Altogether his nap was interrupted three or four more times so that he could keep up with his hungry mother.

When I called it a day at 11 P.M., I was exhausted, but it had been the most absorbing and fascinating day of observing wildlife in my life.

Because the family was usually seen on or near Stony Hill, between the drainages of Big Stony and Little Stony creeks, I began to call the mother bear Big Stony and the cub Little Stony. I learned a lot about bears by watching these two over the next years.

Like all cubs, Little Stony loved to nurse but was often turned down when he asked for milk. As his mother fed, he often sneaked under her belly and tried to nurse. When this happened, she usually walked off, causing him to lose his balance and fall over. Sometimes, if he had a good grip on one of her nipples, he hung on and nursed as he was dragged across the tundra. Occasionally Big Stony swung around and bit him hard enough to make him let go.

As with his persistent attempts to enroll her in play, the cub was not easily deterred from nursing. Again and again he slipped under her stomach and reached up to nurse only to be left behind as she moved off.

When Little Stony got really hungry, he made a whining call that sounded like "waugh." About every two hours, his mother gave Little Stony what he wanted. She chose a spot, sat down, and lay back. He came running, climbed up on her belly, and got busy. As he nursed, he made a buzzing sound. Grizzly sows have six teats, and the little cub went from one teat to another as he drained each. He had to walk back and forth on her belly and chest, and Big Stony often held him in her paws so he wouldn't fall off. Nursing sessions lasted about four minutes. To end them, the sow simply got up and walked away.

Most of the time, the nursing ended before the cub was satisfied, and he pestered her for more. On one occasion, however, Big Stony fell asleep while nursing. For once Little Stony had plenty of time to feed. He made a complete circuit of her teats and drained her dry. Then it was time for a nap. He was so full that he just plopped down on her belly and began snoozing.

As a young cub,
Little Stony likes to stay
close to his mother.

Little Stony is great at climbing up willow bushes. The hard part is figuring out how to climb down.

One of Little Stony's favorite pastimes was willow climbing. As he got better at it, he could work his way ten or fifteen feet up flimsy bushes, using his jaws and front paws to pull himself up. Big Stony seemed to sense the danger in this game and began to pay more attention to his climbing.

One time he was way up in a bush, and she came over and watched him closely. He fell, did a midair flip, and landed at her feet. Immediately, he returned to the willow and climbed back up, even higher than before. He swayed back and forth on a narrow branch near the top, playing to his audience of one. Soon — possibly frightened of the height — he tried to get down. After several false starts and close calls, he finally learned that it was best to reverse directions and climb down head first.

In their travels, the family sometimes encountered other tundra residents. The most common other big animal was the caribou. A healthy adult caribou bull or cow can easily outrun a bear and is so confident of its speed that it often walks by bears with little evident concern. Experienced bears ignore these temptations, for they know it's a waste of energy to chase faster animals.

Little Stony had not yet learned that lesson.

He knew instinctively that caribou were safe targets to charge. Often during that first summer, he chased them across the tundra. His enthusiasm was admirable, but the sight of a little ten-pound cub clumsily galloping after a graceful caribou going forty miles per hour was comical. When he tired, he gave up and trotted back to his mother, who had completely ignored the caribou and chase. In some cases, the caribou jogged back to the bears, perhaps curious, wanting to see what the two were doing. This was too much for the cub to resist. He mounted a second campaign and tried to grab the caribou before it got away. He never caught one, but he did his best — and got a good workout.

Caribou were harmless, but other animals on the tundra wanted to eat little cubs: big male grizzlies (also known as boars). Little Stony knew that other bears were to be feared. When he was six months old, an adult bear ambled onto the scene, suddenly noticed the cub and headed toward him. The cub was fifty feet from his mother. Instantly he streaked over to her and positioned himself behind her so that her body was between him and the oncoming danger. Then he stood up and looked over his mother's back at the approaching bear.

The sow quickly spotted the strange grizzly. Without hesitation she charged him. The boar stood his ground for a moment and assessed the situation. He outweighed her and almost certainly was stronger. In an all-out fight, he would likely be the winner. On the other hand, the mother bear hurtling toward him was committed to

Little Stony watches a strange grizzly approach.

Confident in its ability to outrun bears, a caribou swings over to take a closer look at mother and cub.

fight to the death to protect her cub. Deciding it wasn't worth the risk, the boar turned tail and fled. Big Stony pursued him a short distance before circling back to Little Stony, who was loudly crying out. A nursing session eased his trauma and quieted him down.

Grizzlies in Denali National Park live on a predominantly vegetarian diet. They would undoubtedly love to catch and eat fish, but the park's glacial streams are mainly devoid of them. Since moose,

26

caribou, and Dall sheep are difficult to kill, most grizzlies learn that Arctic ground squirrels offer them their best chance at a high-protein meal. Adult squirrels contain as many as 2,400 calories, a healthy meal for a bear. A research project found that one Alaskan grizzly sow caught and ate three hundred squirrels during the course of a single summer.

Big Stony was a seasoned squirrel catcher, constantly on the alert for them. On seeing one, she immediately rushed it, trying to grab it before it dived into its burrow. If the squirrel reached its home, Big Stony dug after it with relentless persistence, spending as much as thirty minutes excavating a single tunnel.

When his mother caught a squirrel, Little Stony would rush over and demand a piece of it. She never willingly shared a squirrel with him.

When Little Stony was eight months old, Big Stony caught a squirrel and was beginning to eat it. The cub came over and stuck his face inches from her jaws as she chewed. Then he cried out loudly, demanding part of the meal. Ignoring his cry, she turned away and tried to finish the squirrel in peace. He continued to whine and again crowded her as she ate. She dropped the squirrel, growled at the cub, and gave him a good bite on his back. As a result of her punishment, he kept his distance until she finished. After she walked off, he went over and sniffed the inedible parts left behind, mainly the skin and tail. He chewed on them for a while but, except for a little taste,

Arctic ground squirrels are the bears' favorite food, and compared to other prey, easier to catch.

couldn't have gotten much out of them.

As Little Stony got bigger and more experienced, he learned to be more assertive when it came to what he wanted to eat. Just a month after the above incident, mother and cub tried to dig up yet another squirrel. It was late August and an early snowstorm had deposited three inches of snow on the tundra. The sow caught the squirrel after about twenty minutes of work. As always, Little Stony ran over and cried out for his share. She ignored him and continued to eat the delicacy.

Suddenly he lunged for the squirrel, trying to tear it out of her mouth. She retaliated by biting him on the back, but to do so required her to drop the squirrel. For a second, they each stared at the squirrel lying on the ground, then each dived for it simultaneously. Mustering all the force his forty-five-pound body could generate, Little Stony wrestled with his mother over the prize he desperately wanted.

The two bears rolled around in the fresh powder snow, kicking up so much of the stuff it looked like they were in a miniature blizzard. After a half a minute of battle, the cub ran off defeated, having been taught his manners by his powerful mother.

Or so it seemed. When Little Stony had gone fifty feet, he stopped to look back. The squirrel dangled from his mouth. Big Stony glared at him in disgust, then walked off. He had taken a big chance for a highly desired snack and won.

PRECEDING PAGES:
Another nursing session.
Grizzly milk contains
2,300 calories per quart,
and has a fat content
that is as much as eleven
times that found in
human milk. Milk is a
cub's only source of
nutrition from birth in
January through April,
when the family leaves the
winter den. Big Stony
nurses her cub about once
every two hours.

· ·

The next time I saw the sow catch a squirrel, she quickly looked over at her cub. He was digging at another burrow entrance and had his back turned. Without moving or making much of a sound, she quickly gulped her meal whole, dispensing with the usual chewing that prolonged the delicate taste. Just as she swallowed, the cub looked over and realized something was happening. He charged over and looked first at the wrecked burrow and then at his mother. From his

The aftermath of the big fight. Little Stony runs away from his mother with his prize held tightly in his jaws.

31

expression, it seemed as though he knew she had caught the occupant, but he couldn't figure out where she had put it. Big Stony turned and walked off, leaving him with his puzzlement.

By September, it was easy to see that Little Stony was becoming increasingly independent. In late spring, when I first saw him, he didn't like to be more than fifty feet from his mother. Now it was nothing for him to lag several hundred yards behind. He demonstrated his independence one day on Stony Hill when he persisted in digging up a promising squirrel burrow, oblivious to the fact that his mother had continued on. When she was three hundred yards away from the cub, she stopped and looked around for him. Since he was in a gully, she couldn't spot him. She snorted several times to call him. That did no good so she retraced her steps, back to where he was still digging away at the burrow. She sniffed his back and then walked off, apparently expecting him to follow. Little Stony continued digging for the squirrel that only he believed was in the burrow. When his mother got a good distance away and turned and found that he was still not with her, she went back a second time to get his attention. He only gave up his excavation and followed her when he saw the burrow was empty.

In late September I packed my belongings and prepared to drive to California for my winter job as a ranger in Death Valley National Monument. The last time I saw the two bears that year, they were feeding by Little Stony Creek, concentrating on their eating so intently that they failed to see a wolf moving across the tundra toward them.

A squirrel popped out of a burrow and Big Stony gave chase. Her pursuit took her right toward the wolf. By the time she saw him, she was only one hundred yards away. She stopped and looked back and saw that the cub was galloping toward her. He caught up with her and watched the wolf over his mother's shoulder.

Little Stony was still small enough to tempt a wolf. There have been a number of sightings in Denali of wolves stalking cubs. Once a wolf pack separated two yearling cubs from their mother and killed them.

Big Stony stood up and stared at the wolf. She must have presented an intimidating sight, for the wolf quickly left the area.

It had been a great summer for me. I had been able to watch a grizzly family at close range on almost a daily basis. Observing Little Stony and his mother had enabled me to learn more about bears than I had in all my previous summers in Denali. I hoped to return next spring and watch them more. As I left the park that fall I wished them well and hoped that they would enjoy their months in hibernation.

. . . .

When I returned to Denali next spring, six weeks went by without any sign of the two bears. I feared that something had happened to them during hibernation or that a male bear had grabbed the cub.

On July 5, two bears showed up near the road at Stony Hill. They looked like a mother and yearling, but since the cub had

In his second year, Little Stony's fur turns blond. Here, he is surrounded by a patch of his beloved bear flowers.

After Little Stony's relentless taunting and teasing, his mother finally pays attention to him, and they play on the park road, holding up traffic for about ten minutes.

blond fur, it didn't resemble Little Stony. The yearling went up to the sow and smacked her in the face. She turned and walked off. He trotted over to her, swung his right foreleg over her shoulder, and tried to push her over. The two bears wrestled for the next ten minutes. Despite the new fur color, the cub was undeniably Little Stony. He had survived to see his second summer after all.

From then on, they were seen almost every day in their old territory along the park road. Their behavior patterns were much the same as the summer before. The sow spent almost all her time feeding, except for brief nursing sessions and rare playtimes with the cub.

Little Stony was as curious and playful as ever, and he loved to pester his mother. One day he deliberately got in her way as she was eating. After a while, sick of his interruptions, she opened her jaws and lunged at him, missing his rear end by inches. Thrilled by her attention, Little Stony raced down the road with the sow at his heels. They ran several hundred yards, went around a curve, and accidentally scattered three carloads of tourists who stood innocently on the road.

Little Stony showed an increasing interest in the buses and cars that traveled the park road. When the sow crossed the road, she ignored any vehicles that had stopped to watch them. Little Stony, lagging behind as usual, often stopped and looked up at the nearest vehicle.

One day he wandered over to a truck and bit the rubber portion of the front bumper. On other occasions, he sniffed the tires of a van and looked through the closed door of a shuttle bus. He seemed to have no motive other than curiosity, and he always moved on without incident.

The two bears familiarity with the road and shuttle buses was dramatically illustrated one day when they were threatened by a male grizzly. The sow and cub were feeding a few hundred yards south of the road when they saw the other grizzly moving in their direction.

The cub's curiosity becomes directed toward vehicles he sees on the road. Sometimes he walks over to a car and sniffs or bites the bumper. But when he realizes he is lagging behind his mother, he hurries after her.

A squirrel has just slipped under this piece of machinery at a gravel pit. The two bears try to reach in and grab it, but the squirrel is out of their reach.

Deciding that it would be safer to flee, the sow spun around and sprinted for the road with the cub right behind. When they reached the road, she spotted a bus and trotted toward it. They stopped just a few feet from the bus and sat down to rest while they watched the other bear. He had followed them part of the way, but had halted and seemed nervous about approaching the road and especially the bus. After a few moments, he turned around and left the area.

It's impossible to say what was really going on in the sow's mind, but the incident left the impression that she knew the boar was frightened of the bus and she deliberately brought the cub there to make her stand.

The most entertaining show of the summer took place on a hot day in late July. Both sow and cub still had their thick winter coats (which they normally shed from late July through mid-August) and were having a tough time dealing with the unusually warm weather. As they wandered over the tundra, they happened on a small pond and immediately seemed to recognize its potential. They dove into the cool water and swam back and forth across the pond. After a while, the cub grew bored and looked for something new to do in the water.

He swam over to the sow and splashed her in the face. She stood up in the shallow water and jumped at him. He may have been faster on land, but she was a better swimmer, and she quickly caught him and tossed him around, thoroughly soaking him. He broke away from her and tried to swim off, but she caught him again. When he escaped the next time, he managed to make it to land, but once there he immediately turned round and sailed through the air, plunging into

OVERLEAF: A swim on a hot July day turns into a no-holds-barred wrestling match.

39

the water scant inches from his mother's face. They swam, dove, and splashed for much of that afternoon.

As they had the previous summer, the two bears spent a lot of time digging for squirrels. The cub always joined in when he saw his mother start to excavate a tunnel system, but often lost interest within a few minutes. He still wanted the squirrel but didn't like the hard work required to get it. However, he stayed nearby, hoping either to grab the squirrel as it escaped or to steal a captured one from his mother. One time the sow dug such a large hole that both she and the cub fit in it. Little Stony climbed out and amused himself by rolling stones down a hillside. When she later caught the squirrel, he was too busy playing with the rocks to notice, and she ate it without harassment.

Fall came quickly that year. It had been a good summer for berries and both bears put on a lot of weight. The cub looked like he was now around one hundred pounds. By September, his new winter coat of darker fur was beginning to show under the silver-blond outer coat. In late September, the sow and cub found a lamb that had died from a fall. The mother shared the lamb with Little Stony, perhaps because it was big enough for both to eat at once.

Soon it was time for me to move on to my winter job in the desert. The next summer would be critical in the life of the cub because it would be time for him to go it alone.

Now twenty months old, Little Stony rests in a berry patch as his mother continues to feed.

43

YEAR 3 THREE

Not long after I returned to the park the next spring, I had my first sighting of the pair. They were galloping at top speed across the braided channels of the Toklat River. In pursuit was a large male grizzly. Leaping up on the road, the sow paused for a moment and frantically looked around. She and the cub were blocked by a near-vertical cliff rising from the far

Mother and cub asleep following a morning of eating grass.

45

After fleeing from a male bear, the family takes refuge on a high cliff.

side of the road. The other bear was now only a few hundred feet from them. Little Stony pressed up against his mother for protection. The sow then made her decision. She ran across the road and ascended a steep gully that bisected the cliff. The cub followed her without hesitation. Loose shale covered the gully and caused them to slip backward frequently, but they pressed on despite the hindrance.

By the time the boar reached the road, the sow and cub had made it to a rocky pinnacle, two hundred feet above him. He stared up at them and must have decided that further pursuit was unwise, because he walked down the road and disappeared. The two bears, mother and cub, were panting heavily, not yet recovered from the close call. The sow brought things back to normal by leaning back and offering the cub a nursing session. They stayed up on the cliff most of the day, evidently out of fear that the other bear might come back.

Their concern was justified. Recently, at this part of the Toklat River, two cubs had been killed by male bears, perhaps by the same bear. In one case, a bear surprised a sow with twin yearlings. The family tried to run off, but one cub lagged behind and was dealt a crippling blow by the male. The mother bear spun around and attacked him in a desperate attempt to save the yearlings. The boar wouldn't back down and killed her. Her attack and sacrifice enabled the second cub to escape.

· ·

With all the excitement that accompanied that first sighting, I didn't have time to take a close look at the cub. A few weeks later, he and his mother spent several hours near the road and I was better able to renew my acquaintance with him. His fur was long and golden blond. He was now so big that at times it was hard to tell who was the mother and who was the cub. When he ate some grass right next to the road, I noticed that he had a diagonal scar across his forehead. Had he gotten it during a fight with his mother or in an encounter with another bear?

Little Stony and his mother at the start of his third summer. Now two-and-one-half years old, he is so big that it is difficult to tell mother from cub. Notice the scar on the cub's forehead.

47

. . . .

After they fed on grass for an hour or so, the sow moved off a short way and lay on her back. Little Stony ran over and started to nurse. He was now two-and-a-half years old; while it was normal for cubs that age to nurse, it was still a strange sight to see such a big cub nurse. As he fed, the sow dozed off. The cub greedily drank all the milk and then, when he was sure it was all gone, stretched out on top of her and joined her in a nap.

During the coming weeks, I saw them often and noticed that the cub's personality had not changed. One day, he found a snowbank and practiced the sledding techniques he had perfected during his first summer. Another time, while meandering down the road, he found a bright-orange traffic cone and spent ten minutes slapping at it and biting it. He continued to be intrigued by the cars and buses that stopped to watch him.

The last time I saw them together was in July. They were on Stony Hill, hunting for squirrels. The sow caught one and had expertly elbowed Little Stony out of the way when he came over and tried to grab it. All he got was a taste of blood when he licked the spot where the squirrel had been killed. She hurried off at a deliberate pace, and the cub had to rush to keep up with her.

When I failed to see the family for several weeks, I wondered if they had split up. In central Alaska it is normal for grizzly families to

Despite his size, the cub still nurses. Grizzly cubs normally continue to nurse as long as they are with their mothers. OVERLEAF: On finishing his milk, Little Stony dozes off on top of his mother, just as he had done during his first year.

Still intensely curious and playful, the cub loves to investigate objects, such as this traffic cone. RIGHT: Since the family often feeds next to the park road, they give thousands of people their first close-up view of grizzly bears.

separate when the cubs are two-and-a-half years old. The mother is ready to breed again and must drive her cubs away before male bears will court her. If she doesn't, the cubs may be looked upon as rivals and attacked.

Although no one witnessed the Big Stony-Little Stony split, based on other observations of grizzly families, the process went something like this. The mother's milk supply would dry up first, making their relationship strained and tense. A moment would come when the sow would turn on the cub and attack him. At first he might think it was

A snowbank is not only a great place to cool off on a hot day, but it also provides the cub with an opportunity to practice his skiing.

another game, but the attack would persist until he fled from her reach. From then on, whenever he tried to approach her, the sow would charge him.

It would have taken a while, but eventually Little Stony would have grasped the idea that he wasn't wanted by his mother any longer. The split must have been very traumatic. For his entire life up to that

LEFT: Little Stony on his own for the first time.
ABOVE: Big Stony sleeping. She cannot allow her cub to stay with her any longer.

moment, his mother had fed and protected him. Now, for reasons unknown to him, she was rejecting him. And, while he didn't realize it, he would be alone for the rest of his life.

In late July, I photographed a bear feeding by the side of the road. He was there for only a few moments before turning and walking away. I had been so involved with my camera settings that I didn't get a good look at him. When the processed slides came back later, I saw that he had a scar on his forehead. It had been Little Stony, now clearly on his own.

As the summer moved into August, he frequently showed up in the highway pass and Toklat River area, the eastern end of his mother's home range. He looked more and more like an adult grizzly, probably weighing around two hundred pounds, and his coat was now black and sleek. In personality, however, he was the same as ever. Whenever he found a traffic cone, Park Service sign, or surveyor's stake, he couldn't resist playing with it. His travels often took him near the road and he exhibited the same curiosity toward cars and buses.

That year the Park Service hired a private contractor to build a pair of bridges across the Toklat River. As a condition of the contract, the construction company was instructed to dispose of its garbage in bear-proof containers. The local law-enforcement rangers kept an eye on the construction site, especially on the garbage containers.

AREA CLOSED
CRITICAL
WILDLIFE HABITAT

Now that he is a lone bear, Stony has more time to examine interesting objects such as Park Service signs.

A surveyor's stake at the Toklat Bridge construction site serves as a scratching post.

Stony's normal route often took him near the construction site, and all the strange objects he saw there frequently aroused his extraordinary curiosity. When he passed through the area, he sometimes paused and sniffed fuel barrels, lumber piles, and pieces of heavy equipment. He never threatened or got too close to any of the workers. During the times he was in the area, the crew members climbed into the nearest vehicle or other shelter and waited until he left.

Late one day, Stony approached the construction site and sniffed his way through the area. He eventually came across a plastic garbage

· ·

can, one that wasn't bear-proof. It had a smell he was especially interested in. He smacked its side, knocked it over, and scattered its contents over the ground. Mixed in with a few oil cans, empty beer cans, rags, antifreeze containers, and scraps of lumber were the remains of five sack lunches. Pawing through the garbage, Stony quickly found the leftovers and wolfed them down. The construction workers tried to scare him off by yelling, but he wouldn't leave.

Brad Ebel, the local Park Service road-crew foreman, drove by and saw the bear eating out of the can. He used his radio to call Jim Schlinkmann, the Toklat patrol ranger, and told him about the situation. Fortunately, Jim was nearby and arrived on the scene a few minutes later. Stony was still rooting through the contents of the overturned can, hoping to find more food. Jim drove into the site and pulled near the can, where he turned on his siren and scared the bear away from the can.

The bear wandered through other parts of the construction site and investigated other piles of discarded material. He found a roll of insulation, tore off a small piece, and ate it. Later he returned to the trash can, but by then all the food had been taken away.

Jim talked to the owner of the company, reiterated in strong terms the need to put all food in bear-proof garbage containers, and gave him a citation for violation of food-storage restrictions. He also

Stony tries but fails to break into this Park Service bear-resistant garbage can.

told him to expect a full inspection of the site in the morning. The area was cleaned up and from then on all food was apparently disposed of properly. We hoped this incident would be an isolated one, and that Stony would not look for more food in other garbage cans.

The next day, as I approached a rest stop a mile east of Toklat, I saw that a large number of cars and buses had stopped. People had their cameras out and were photographing something at the rest stop. When I got closer, I saw that the center of attention was a grizzly trying to break into a Park Service garbage can. I had a sinking feeling that it was Stony. A moment later the bear turned in my direction: he had a scar on his forehead. This type of garbage can was designed to resist break-ins by grizzlies, and it stood up well to Stony's assault. All he could do was rip off a part of the black plastic liner that stuck out of the can.

To the tourists who watched him try to get into the can, it must have seemed like a great show. Each time he ripped a new piece of plastic liner, everyone laughed. When Stony finally walked off, each person excitedly talked about how funny it was to see the bear try to get into the garbage can. I knew differently. This was now serious — it looked like Stony was falling into a pattern of seeking out food in garbage cans.

A few weeks after this incident, I packed my belongings and was

OVERLEAF: By the end of his third summer, Stony begins to be led astray by his curious personality. He is still a wild grizzly, but he shows too much interest in humans and their things.

preparing to leave the park. Realizing that I had left my hat at the Toklat Road Camp, a Park Service residential area, I went to retrieve it. When I pulled into the camp, I saw Jim Schlinkmann and he told me that Stony was in the area and had tried to approach the big trash compactor that held all the Park Service garbage. The compactor was bear-proof, but we didn't want Stony to hang around the area so we tried to figure out how to scare him off.

A short time later, he appeared on the Toklat River bar, heading for the camp. We positioned our vehicles between him and the compactor. The patrol car and my truck presented enough of a barrier to cause him to stop. He looked over at the camp, then started to paw at the ground, attempting to dig up some edible roots. After a while he moved off and tried to approach the camp from a different angle. We were able to block that route too, and he went back to digging roots. Jim had to leave, but he asked me to stay and try to keep Stony away.

For the next few hours, it was just he and I. His pattern was the same: he dug roots for ten or twenty minutes and then tried to get into the camp from a new direction; I moved my truck and blocked his access.

There were many times during those hours when he was only a few yards from my truck. During those moments, he stared me right in the eye and I stared back at him. His eyes had the same look I had seen when I watched him as a newborn cub, only two-and-a-half years ago. The look revealed a grizzly that was intensely curious about his surroundings and that loved to investigate whatever he came across.

Those traits were acceptable in most circumstances, but they now brought him to a point where he might become addicted to human food. Those sack lunches had tasted far better than roots and grass — and he wanted more. His future would depend on whether he continued to pursue this path. When he finally left the area, I pulled out of the camp and headed out of the park. Throughout the coming winter, I thought often about Stony and what would become of him.

YEAR 4 FOUR

. . . .

The following spring came and I returned to the park. It was late June when I first saw Stony. He was on the east side of Stony Hill, digging for squirrels. His fur had turned blond again, but he still had his scar, making it easy to identify him.

On that first day he started to cross the road, noticed my truck, walked over and bit the

Stony playing with a rubber casing protecting an elevation marker.

67

· ·

Mileposts on the park road need to be inspected.

front bumper. Continuing on, he spotted a plastic milepost sign and batted it back and forth with his paw. Later he found a rubber casing that protected a U.S. Geological Service bench marker, and he played with it for a few minutes. His curiosity had certainly not diminished.

In the coming days, he spent most of his time feeding near the road. All in all, he was a well-behaved bear. He stayed away from garbage cans and other sources of temptation. It looked like he was back on course.

On July 5, I saw two men photographing a bear near Big Stony Creek. The men were about one hundred feet off the road and the grizzly was about two hundred feet beyond them. Since they had a professional photographer's permit and the terms of the permit prohibited them from leaving the road to approach a bear, I called them back. As they picked up their tripods and cameras, I looked at the bear through my binoculars and saw that it was Stony. He had seemed indifferent to their approach and continued feeding as the photographers returned to the road.

About two hours later, while working in the Eielson Visitor Center, I heard a series of transmissions on the park radio about a bear mauling near Big Stony Creek. From the initial reports, it seemed a bear had approached a hiker and bitten him on the leg. The injured man had later walked to the road and was now being treated for his wounds. He said the bear that attacked him was blond and had a scar on his forehead. Only one bear matched that description.

My duties kept me at the visitor center for the next few hours. A number of law enforcement and bear-management rangers headed out to the scene of the incident. News of the mauling spread among the visitors and they all asked about it.

The hiker told rangers that he had been photographing the bear when it began to close in on him, stopping only a few feet away. It leaned forward and sniffed his tripod and then his elbow. The hiker flinched, which startled the bear and caused it to back off a few yards. At that point, the hiker dropped to the ground and played dead. He said that he sensed the bear come up to him, sniff his leg, and then it pulled on his pant leg and boot. Finally, he said, the bear bit into his calf and then licked the blood. While still lying down, the hiker tried to slip his pack off. This motion seemed to scare the bear, and it backed off. After a moment it started to graze. Deciding that he should try to get away, the hiker stood and limped out to the road. The bear continued to move away and did not bother him any further.

By now, several shuttle buses had arrived at Eielson, containing people who had witnessed part of the incident. I talked to some of them and found that their accounts shed some new light on the events leading up to the attack. The witnesses said that they first saw the hiker walking around some distance from his camp. He noticed the bear, rushed back to his tent, and returned with a camera and tripod. He was seen moving closer to the bear as he photographed it, carrying his tripod along with him. At the same time, the bear fed in a pattern that brought him toward the hiker. When the bear noticed the hiker, it stopped feeding and looked at him. At this point they were about fifty yards apart.

The witnesses then saw the bear turn sideways and hunch up, a gesture that, among bears, is intended to scare off a threatening rival. Turning the opposite way, it repeated the action. Next it paced back and forth in a line parallel to the hiker, another display whose purpose is to drive off a rival. The hiker stayed put, a response that may have been the reason the bear suddenly charged forward. Stopping about fifteen yards away, it again hunched up and appeared to curl its lips back. A few moments later, it walked off a short distance and went back to grazing.

A bit later the bear looked back, saw that the hiker was still in the area, and began walking back toward him. Some witnesses reported that the hiker sat down fifteen to twenty feet in front of his camera setup, which made them wonder if he was trying to get a time-released shot of himself and the bear in the same frame.

When I was finished at the visitor center, I rushed over to the

scene of the incident. Stony could still be seen off in the distance, quietly feeding on the tundra as if nothing had happened. Around ten other rangers and park employees were there discussing what should be done about him. One ranger felt he should be destroyed or captured and moved out of the area. He felt that this attack, combined with the bear's past history of interest in human food, made it too

After the incident with the hiker, two rangers approach Stony to test his response to people. In this test and others, he either ignores the rangers or moves away from them.

(continued on page 76)

What to Do When You Encounter a Grizzly

Anytime you hike in grizzly country, you must be prepared for the possibility that one might charge you. In Denali and many other areas containing grizzlies, hiking is often done in fairly open terrain. In these areas, watch for bears and change your route if you see one ahead. When walking through brushy territory, make a lot of noise so that any nearby bears can be alerted to your presence. Most grizzlies prefer to avoid people, and by giving one advance warning, there is a good chance it will move off and not bother you.

If you have accidentally gotten close to a bear, stand still or slowly back away. Never run from a bear, for bears instinctively chase running prey. Talking to it in a low, soothing voice may help it to realize that you mean it no harm. In the event the bear moves toward you, yell and wave your arms. Grizzly eyesight is poor and it's possible that it may not have identified you as a human. Yelling and arm waving help the bear to classify you correctly. If the bear continues to come closer and looks like it is going to attack, drop to the ground and play dead. When grizzlies attack people, it is almost always because they feel threatened. By playing dead, you stand a good chance of convincing the bear that you are no longer a threat.

In the incident involving Stony, the hiker had a number of choices, many of which probably would have saved him from injury. Obviously, he never should have approached the bear in the first place. When Stony began to display defensive behavior, the hiker should have backed away. Once Stony moved toward him, he might have been able to drive him off by yelling and waving his arms. Playing dead is the last option. The fact that Stony backed off when the hiker tried to take his pack off indicates that the bear could have been scared off much earlier.

In his fourth summer, Stony's fur returns to a blond color.

risky to allow him to live or stay where he would encounter other people. Others in the group felt strongly that the bear had been provoked and was not to blame. I tried to explain Stony's history and argued that his actions were based primarily on curiosity rather than intent to harm. (A park ranger later interviewed the hiker and his conclusion mirrored mine.)

Stony's fate was decided by park superintendent Clay Cunningham. After reviewing the case, he instructed the bear-management rangers to tranquilize Stony, put a radio collar on him, and give him another chance.

In past years when bears caused problems in national parks such as Denali, Yellowstone, Yosemite, and Sequoia, they were often shot. More recent Park Service policies have experimented with using negative conditioning as a way of changing a problem bear's behavior.

During the next several days, a number of conditioning tests were performed on Stony. Most of the tests involved having two armed rangers deliberately approach him. They monitored his reaction, and if he threatened or moved toward them, they fired rubber bullets or cracker shells toward him. This latter type of projectile contained a firecrackerlike charge that exploded with a lot of noise but little power. Both the rubber bullets and cracker shells were designed to teach him to fear humans without inflicting serious injury on the bear.

. . . .

Stony did well on the tests. When approached, he made no attempt to move toward the rangers. He either ignored them or slowly walked away. In one test the rangers intentionally got in his path. Stony saw them and moved aside to avoid them. The rangers never needed to use the rubber bullets or cracker shells. So far, it looked good for him.

A few weeks later, he encountered another temptation. Two hikers left their backpacks on the side of the road and walked off to take some pictures. While they were gone, Stony happened by and saw the packs. He sniffed them and bit into one of the sleeping pads, but made no effort to get at the food inside the packs. That he ignored the food was another positive sign.

Stony was now officially known as bear No. 115, a number assigned to him when he was drugged and fitted with a radio collar. At the same time, a numbered tag was placed in each ear so that he could be identified if he slipped his collar. Throughout the rest of the summer I cringed every time I saw him with his radio collar and tags. His accessories branded him a bad bear, a label I hated to see hung on him.

Without making a conscious choice, I stopped taking pictures of him. I didn't want any shots of him wearing the undignified tags and collar. I hoped that he would continue to behave and that the offensive items would be removed subsequently.

YEAR 5 FIVE

. . . .

The next summer, my first sighting of Stony occurred in early June. He still had his radio collar and ear tags, but his fur had turned brown. I had been watching a mother bear with twin cubs when Stony came on the scene. The sow stood up, looked at him, then fled with her cubs. Stony followed them for a distance, but when he crossed

Finding a Dall sheep ewe that died of natural causes, Stony makes full use of the carcass.

79

the road, he was distracted by some vehicles. After investigating the cars, he fed near the road. As he did, the sow and cubs watched from about three hundred yards away. The cubs were nervous and only calmed down when allowed to nurse.

About ten minutes later, Stony walked toward them. Both cubs ran behind their mother for protection. The sow then went into action; she charged Stony, who immediately turned and ran off. After chasing him for a few minutes, she trotted back to her cubs. As soon as she reversed directions, Stony turned back and again approached the family. The mother bear charged again and drove him away. This

routine repeated itself two more times, and each time the sow seemed to get angrier. Once Stony had been chased off for the fourth time, he lost interest in the family and wandered off. The mother joined her cubs, who were frantic.

After the incident was over, I wondered about his intentions. Had he approached the family so that he could kill one of the cubs or was this just another aspect of his playful, curious nature? The mother and cubs certainly believed he was a threat and acted accordingly.

For a while during his fifth summer, Stony's life seemed to be going well. He stayed away from garbage cans and hikers. His diet

The mother bear on the left places herself between her cubs and Stony before driving him away. He returns several times, but is repeatedly chased off by the enraged sow.

Due to teamwork, wolf packs have much greater success killing caribou than do lone grizzlies.

consisted of the things "good" bears should eat: roots, grass, and ground squirrels. In midsummer, he found a ewe that had died of natural causes and made several meals from its carcass.

Around that time, he made another lucky discovery. A pack of wolves had killed a caribou on Stony Hill. After stuffing themselves as full as they could, they walked off a few hundred yards, and lay down to nap. An hour later Stony wandered by and noticed the wolves. He charged into the pack and sent them running. The wolves ran off, but were too full to go far. They soon stopped and looked back at Stony. By then he was sniffing the air with a great deal of interest. Turning to the west, he trotted off and followed the scent directly to the carcass. Within a few hours, he finished it off. The wolf pack watched him, but didn't do anything to drive him away.

By the middle of August, Stony had left his usual domain around Stony Hill and had begun to head west. On August 20, he was seen about twenty-five miles away, just south of Wonder Lake. He was tranquilized again and had his radio collar replaced. The rangers who handled him estimated his weight at 280 pounds, a good-sized bear by local standards.

I saw him feeding on berries near the Wonder Lake campground a few weeks later. That year the berry crop was poor, but the area around Wonder Lake had produced a decent number of blueberries.

An Arctic ground squirrel standing amid fall colors on the tundra. RIGHT: Mount McKinley and the tundra near Wonder Lake. In the fall of Stony's fifth year, he heads west through this area in search of berry patches.

Perhaps Stony had drifted out of his normal range looking for better berry patches and ended up there.

After I left the area to return to Eielson, Stony headed toward the north end of the lake. That route took him near the Wonder Lake ranger station, an old house used as a residence and office. Behind the station were several small cabins that housed additional employees. Rorie Hammel was doing some chores in one of the cabins; her husband, Rob, the local Park Service grader operator, was out working. Their children, three-year-old Raina and nine-month-old Ryan, were outside playing. Rorie went out to check on the kids, and just as she reached them she saw Stony approaching the station.

They rushed back to their cabin. Once safely inside, they watched the bear through a window. Stony sniffed around the ranger station and then continued on, passing within a few feet of their window. He paused on the north side of the cabin and went up to Raina's little plastic swimming pool. In Raina's own words:

"We heard a big 'whoomph' and I asked Mom, 'What happened, what happened?' I climbed up on the bed, looked outside and saw the bear by my swimming pool. The air was going out, the bear had bit it! I looked again and saw him inside the pool, playing and rolling around in the water. Then he wandered off and went toward the mountain. We went outside and looked at the pool. The pool looked

like it had exploded, it was flat on the ground. There were many tiny pieces of plastic all over."

After he was done playing with the pool, Stony walked over to the road and continued north, past Wonder Lake and on into Kantishna, an old gold-mining district that was added to the park in 1980. Several miles up the road, he paused at the entrance to Camp Denali and scratched himself on a post. Once finished, he went back to the road and walked on. A short time later, he came to the Kantishna Roadhouse. This was a new tourist resort built on a piece of property that had been the center of Kantishna back in the early 1900s, when the area was at the peak of a gold rush.

As Stony walked into the area, he sniffed the air and made a beeline for the Roadhouse garbage dump. He rooted around and found more than enough to make a good meal.

The Roadhouse employees told the Wonder Lake rangers about the bear and they passed the word on to Dave Albert and Joe Van Horn, two rangers who specialized in bear management. Dave was the first to arrive on the scene. By then, Stony was sniffing the air around the Roadhouse kitchen. Dave shot two cracker rounds at Stony, which frightened him enough to move a short distance out of the camp. The bear was reluctant to leave and circled the area. A short time later, he was seen sniffing around the dump again. This time he was hit with a rubber bullet, which caused him to move over to the opposite side of a nearby creek.

For the rest of the day, Stony continually tried to get back to the dump. Dave used rubber bullets and cracker shells to scare him off, but they were becoming increasingly ineffective. A heavier projectile called a "bear thumper" was tried, but it also had little effect. Stony was determined to get back in the dump one way or another.

The next day he found a pickup truck that had several bags of dog food in its bed. Stony climbed into the truck and ate part of the dog food. After being scared off, he circled the area and found a nearby trailer. He smashed through the front door, trashed the inside of the trailer, and then exited by crashing through a kitchen window and leaping to the ground. He returned to the Roadhouse, where he sneaked back to the pickup and tried to eat more dog food. Dave found him there at 11 P.M. and drove him away. The Roadhouse dogs barked all night, indicating that Stony was close by.

The following day, September 14, Stony was first seen at 6 A.M., tearing apart some empty dog-food bags. All morning he stayed near the dump. Joe Van Horn came out to the area and he and Dave Albert did everything they could think of to drive off Stony. They were running out of options.

I'd heard about Stony's adventure over the CB, and since it was

OVERLEAF: Portrait of a grizzly who found it hard to resist certain temptations.

my day off, I went out to Kantishna. Joe filled me in on Stony's actions of the past two days. At that point he was nowhere in sight, so Joe turned on the radio receiver and picked up the signal from Stony's collar. It looked like he was resting in the woods to the south of the dump. Since things were quiet, I walked over to the trailer Stony had broken into. The owner gave me permission to go inside. It looked like vandals had torn apart everything in the living room. The gaping hole in the front door was matched by a bear-sized hole in the kitchen window.

Things looked bleak for Stony. He had gone on a rampage and still hadn't left the area. Breaking into the trailer was a serious offense. Also, he was getting used to the rubber bullets and cracker shells, and their effectiveness was now minimal.

When I got back to Joe, he told me that Stony was still off in the brush and things were quiet. He was going to wait near the dump to see if the bear came back. If Stony did, he said they might decide to drug him and try relocating him to a distant section of the park.

Relocating problem grizzlies has been a common management practice in many national parks. A relocation is an attempt to give a bear another chance in a new area, far removed from garbage and other temptations. Unfortunately, most relocations fail because the bears return home. Once a garbage-addicted bear knows where a good source of food lies, it will quickly return to it once the drugs wear off.

This would most likely be the case with Stony. He had enjoyed some great meals from the Roadhouse dump and from the bags of dog food. He wouldn't let a few days of travel deter him from going back for more. If he came back, there wouldn't be much that could be done. In Alaska, it is legal to shoot a grizzly in defense of life and property. After Stony broke into the trailer, anyone in Kantishna was within his rights to shoot Stony if he approached his property.

The last thing I wanted was to have Stony die from being shot while digging up garbage, but at the moment it looked like that might be his fate. I thought about the possibility of offering him to a zoo. At least it would be a fate better than to be shot in a garbage dump.

Stony was tranquilized later that day and loaded into a helicopter. He was dropped off near the Foraker River, in the western end of the park. All of us who knew Stony waited to see if he would stay there or come back to Kantishna.

The next day, the park plane passed over the relocation area and picked up Stony's radio signal. It seemed to be coming from the exact spot where he had been dropped off. When the crew passed over the area, they saw him lying on the ground, apparently still unconscious from the drug. He should have revived by now. Something was wrong.

EPILOGUE

. . . .

The plane couldn't land and the helicopter was unavailable. A week later, the copter returned and Joe Van Horn was flown out to investigate. Stony had been dead for a week and had been partially eaten by another grizzly. Since the drug dosage he'd received was in the normal range for a bear of his weight, it seemed unlikely that the cause

The new family during a nursing session.

93

of death was an overdose. Joe concluded that Stony may have regurgitated while unconscious and choked to death.

News of Stony's fate quickly spread throughout the park. Initially, I was angry over his death but gradually came to realize that it may have been the lesser of two evils. Had he revived, he almost certainly would have gone straight back to Kantishna.

At least Stony died in wild grizzly country, without pain and with some dignity. The fact that another bear ate part of his carcass may sound distasteful, but it means part of him lives on in the Denali ecosystem.

Stony's life is an apt illustration of the basic conflict built into the mission of the National Park Service. When the agency was created in 1916, Congress stated that its purpose in managing national parks was "to conserve the scenery and the natural and historic objects and the wildlife therein and to provide for the enjoyment of the same in such manner and by such means as will leave them unimpaired for the enjoyment of future generations."

Conflict arises over the relationship between conserving wildlife and natural features and managing the ways people enjoy those resources. That relationship must be balanced in such a way that the animals and natural resources are preserved for the future. It's not an easy task.

Denali National Park was created to protect the wide array of large mammals that live in the area. To help visitors see and enjoy the

. . . .

wildlife, the eighty-five-mile park road was built in the thirties. The road makes the grizzlies and other animals far more accessible to people. On an average summer day, thousands of tourists get to see bears, often within a few feet of their bus. Without the road, only a few backpackers would be able to get a close look at the park's wildlife.

But the road and other developments, which are intended to help people enjoy the wildlife, can be detrimental to the very animals that the park was created to protect. In Stony's case, the traffic on the road and the bridge construction project were sources of temptation that eventually led him astray.

Stony's personality made him curious about human-related objects, particularly food. If Denali had been established solely as a wildlife sanctuary and had no mandate to provide access to the animals, there would have been no road, no construction site, no resorts. Under those circumstances, Stony would have lived in an environment that offered few temptations and he might still be alive today.

But the Park Service mission in Denali is to provide for reasonable access to the park as well as to protect the animals. The trick is to manage the developments that enable access in such a way that the wildlife is left as unimpaired as possible. For the most part, things work in Denali. Unfortunately, Stony's life is an example of how things can go wrong.

Stony's half-sister yawning.

95

No one ever intentionally did anything to harm him, but the chain of events that started with an unsecured trash can, continued with the incident involving the hiker, and ended with a garbage dump, shows how the system could not protect this particular bear.

* * *

Big Stony is still around and doing well. She mated again and gave birth to a pair of female cubs. These half-sisters of Little Stony are now two years old. Both of the new cubs are more wary than he was of people and their things. Also, they have each other to play with, a factor that seemingly has helped them develop into well-adjusted young bears. They have so much fun playing together that their mother often comes over and joins them. Big Stony has become a more attentive and involved mother.

This coming year the family will split up. The cubs, like Little Stony, will probably stay near their mother's home range. If you visit Denali, watch for grizzlies in the Stony Hill area. When you see one, there is a good chance it will be Little Stony's mother or one of his sisters. The sight of one of his close relatives will be an event tens of thousands of people will experience in the coming years. While one bear may have been lost, the rest of the Denali grizzly population is thriving. May those bears continue to live their lives in a truly wild manner.

LEFT: The new cubs watch life go by as they wait for their mother to finish a nap.
ABOVE: A good soapberry crop helps the new cubs to grow quickly during their second summer.

LEFT: Big Stony seems to be more attentive to her cubs. Perhaps experience has made her a better mother. The twins are more wary of people and vehicles than their older brother.
ABOVE: Having each other to play with, the twins are seldom bored.

One of the new cubs watches as a female grizzly passes.

LEFT: The start of another play period.
BELOW: The twins at twenty months. By the time this book is published, they will be on their own. It is not unusual for twin grizzlies to stay together after they leave their mother. Sometimes they even share a den. Sooner or later, however, they will go their separate ways and be solitary animals.

The Denali Foundation Grizzly Fund

The Denali Foundation, a nonprofit environmental organization based in Alaska, has established a special account to fund projects beneficial to grizzly bears and projects that will educate the public about grizzlies.

The author is donating part of his income from sales of this book to the Denali Foundation Grizzly Fund. The Alaska Natural History Association (Denali Branch) will contribute part of their profits from sales of this book to The Denali Foundation. ARA Denali National Park, and ARA Leisure Services Company, the Denali National Park concessionaire and operator of the McKinley Chalet Resort and McKinley Village Lodge, will also donate a percentage of their profits from sales of this book to the Grizzly Fund.

If you would like more information on the Denali Foundation Grizzly Fund or would like to contribute to it, please write:

The Denali Foundation Grizzly Fund, Box 212
Denali Park, Alaska
99755

Readers of *Grizzly Cub: Five Years in the Life of a Bear* can look to Alaska Northwest Books™ for more fascinating accounts of the real-life adventures of bears:

Toklat, The Story of an Alaskan Grizzly Bear,
by Elma and Alfred Milotte, with illustrations by Laura Dassow
The authors spent more than thirty years observing wild animals and filming for Disney True Life Adventures. In *Toklat* they tell the true story of a mother grizzly and her three cubs living through four seasons. Readers of all ages will enjoy this tale.

114 pages, paperback, $9.95 ($12.65 Canadian)   ISBN 0-88240-325-7

Alaska Bear Tales, by Larry Kaniut
Anyone living or traveling in the Alaskan bush knows of the ever-present danger of being attacked by a bear. This best-selling book is a sometimes chilling, always gripping collection of true stories about folks who survived close calls with bears, and those who didn't.

318 pages, paperback, $12.95 ($15.95 Canadian)   ISBN 0-88240-232-3

More Alaska Bear Tales, by Larry Kaniut
Naturalist and storyteller Larry Kaniut offers a page-turning sequel to his best-selling *Alaska Bear Tales.* Once again, the most powerful animal roaming the North American wilderness is front and center, leaving the reader to decide whether the grizzly is a cuddly ball of fur or a frightening predator.

295 pages, paperback, $12.95 ($15.95 Canadian)   ISBN 0-88240-372-9

Ask for these books at your favorite bookstore, or contact Alaska Northwest Books™ for a free catalog of our entire list.

ALASKA NORTHWEST BOOKS™
A division of GTE Discovery Publications, Inc.
P.O. Box 3007
Bothell, WA 98041-2007
Toll free: 1-800-343-4567